NATURE'S VOICE

poetry *Pt* today

NATURE'S VOICE

Edited by Suzy Walton

First published in Great Britain in 2000 by Poetry
Today, an imprint of
Penhaligon Page Ltd, Remus House, Coltsfoot Drive,
Woodston, Peterborough. PE2 9JX

A Catalogue record for this book is available from the
British Library

ISBN 1 86226 601 8

Typesetting and layout, Penhaligon Page Ltd, England.
Printed and bound by Forward Press Ltd, England

Foreword

Nature's Voice is a compilation of poetry, featuring some of our finest poets. This book gives an insight into the essence of modern living and deals with the reality of life today. We think we have created an anthology with a universal appeal.

There are many technical aspects to the writing of poetry and *Nature's Voice* contains free verse and examples of more structured work from a wealth of talented poets.

Poetry is a coat of many colours. Today's poets write in a limitless array of styles: traditional rhyming poetry is as alive and kicking today as modern free verse. Language ranges from easily accessible to intricate and elusive.

Poems have a lot to offer in our fast-paced 'instant' world. Reading poems gives us an opportunity to sit back and explore ourselves and the world around us.

Contents

Tempus Fugit

The book of well-loved country walks
Sleeps snugly on the shelf,
Its pages browned and lifeless,
Inert, in dubious health,
A mirror of its owner,
Like it, seen better days,
Who travelled down lush country trails,
And dark, mysterious ways.
A frayed, forgotten haversack
Flops, lifeless, none forlorner,
And faded, care-worn walking boots
Stay idly in the corner.
A decorated walking-stick
Stands ready in the hall,
Upright, tall and polished,
To wait the master's call.
That call is never coming,
The word not on his lips,
The aged, immobile traveller
Has stale arthritic hips.
Yet still, in memory's golden haze,
He dreams of Samarkand,
And travels the forbidden trails,
And views the promised land.
Alas the book of walks is closed,
Oiled jacket now in hock,
The only journey he makes now
Is once around the block.

Jack Scrafton

Twilight

O soft the air, still warm the shade,
When arched branches of weeping willow,
Gracefully sway in twilight's glade,
Gentle now the breeze, and aerial the place,
That has weaved your willow garland,
Of memories face.
The soft murmur of trees, and the skylarks song,
Shall lift your spirit to where peace belongs.
And wild summer flowers in splendid array,
Shall perfume your path along Elysian's way;
The many wayside flowers that we used to know,
And wild honeysuckle and musk rose,
Under the warm summer's glow.
And those weeping branches of silvery leaves,
Still sway, in the warm twilight's breeze,
While all around an elusive enchanting power,
Shall breathe through the breath,
Of each fragrant bower.

Christine Hare

Here And Now

How lucky are we who live in England
For no matter which town is yours
We don't need to travel but two miles out
To be in the great outdoors

Towns may seem to run together
But we are protected by laws
From building all over our beautiful land
So we can enjoy the outdoors

Outdoors to me is the smell of cut grass
Newly cut to control the weeds
For grass makes a backdrop wherever you are
For all kinds of flowers and seeds

Seeds fall this year to rest until next
But this year's flowers are here
With some it's the shape of the bloom head
And the scent on some has no peer

Any seeds that are left will not go to waste
Our wild creatures will seek them out
To build up their fat layers ready to face
The cold snow that may come about

The sad thought for me as I go through my life
Is that during life's careless way
I may lose my sight or my sense of smell
But I'm here now to enjoy this day.

Sheila Bates

Afterthought

A walk in the sun just to lighten the blues,
I take it all in as I lace up my shoes,
Where once there were skylarks and songthrushes plenty,
Their absence is evident and the airways are empty.
They're not the first and they won't be the last,
Neglect and greed makes them a thing of the past.
Pesticides, insecticides, if there's cash we can sell it,
Large scale weedkillers to the tiny slug pellet.
It's all for the good and our children's inheritance,
By the time they're like me it's more than a penance.
So let's go fishing and hurry with haste,
As we tip-toe around washed-up barrels of toxic waste.
We might catch something called a cod with this hook,
But if we fail there's always one here in this book.
I shudder at the thought of this daytime nightmare,
Then turn ourselves around, just to show that we care.

John Gallen

Nature Simples

In nature ~ lies a truth
Not concrete trivia of phone or TV
Perhaps in there lies illusion
My truth comes through trees.

As if opening my eyes
Or leaving a darkest room
Seeing a bird or crisp insect
It occurs to me that all is well.

Whichever material concerns or worry
Once had, is not real, a film
Only a grass shows how things are
Watching a creature cling to a blade in the breeze.

Simple, small things please me here
Away from blinding noise, see clear
As nature now feeds me, wraps me up
In real things, not concrete but energy.

Feel the prickly, smooth and petal
Chewing wild herbs like living lessons
Nature nurturing me, showing the way
How am I clueless away from you?

Susan Karen Bridges

A Summer's Day

I saw the sun arise this morning.
With rapturous glow the day was dawning.
Song birds sweet chorus filled the air.
Petals unfolded with beauty so fair.
Rainbowed dewdrops on the grass so green.
God gave us freely this wonderful scene.

I saw dark clouds on the hills at noon.
Sure enough the storm came soon.
First the flash and then the crash.
Pitter patter, clatter clatter came the
rain, making rapid rivers down the lane.
Trees and bushes, plants and flowers,
drank joyfully after long dry hours.

I saw the moon rise up at night.
Her silver beams gave glorious light.
Above the lakes she sailed so high
in a soft velvet blue and diamond sky.
With iridescent glow the earth she covered.
This night was made for nature lovers.

Later as I lay in bed,
pictures flashed inside my head.
Then slowly, I began to
dream, of all the miracles in one day
I'd seen.

Barbara Bradley

The Call Of Nature

The call of nature
is out there
the whereabouts
can be seen from
hedgerows paraded around
a field
to fields of wheat
all folded neat.

The call of nature
beckons me to leafy lanes
all shaded green to rural
paths giving right of way
to pastures new all around
the countryside.

Now a memory is all
that remains of summer days
spent down country lanes
I once walked until I
return one summer's day.

Ernest Cummings

The Great Outdoors

Trees sway gently in the breeze,
Wild flowers' petals attract the bees,
Rabbits scamper among the thistles with their powerful legs,
While a mother bird sits upon her eggs,
Mice freeze as a fox comes by,
As a bear licks her cubs with a happy sigh,
Hedgehogs sniff in the fallen leaves,
Owls rest up high in the trees,
As it gets darker some animals sleep,
But as for the owls it's a midnight treat,
Bats fly around as the animals rest,
But in the farm there's an uninvited guest.

Emma Armitage (13)

The Skylark

My boots waxed, lyrical, upon the heaving earth,
The sense of freedom astounding,
And we were close,
So very close,
The mountain and myself.
But now I lie here,
Amongst the rock and lichen,
My shattered legs beneath me,
And high upon the sunlight
Sings a skylark.
How small a shrug the mountain gave,
To send me reeling,
But I am contented deeply;
Because we are no longer merely close
But one,
The mountain and myself,
And I am high up with the skylark,
And there is sunlight all around me.

Peter C Fry

Willows

Along the road, eight willows stand.
The wind it makes them bend and bend.
They bend one way, go all together.
Which way they bend, is up to the weather.
They stand so proud,
    When the sun is bright.
They protect each other,
    Throughout the night.
It's like a big family they are,
    They wave at people going far.
While here they stand just quite content.
While winds it makes them bend and bend.
They sound they make,
    When winds them heave,
Is quite a noise beyond belief.
Sometimes the worry,
    Will they break?
In autumn their leaves blow o'er the lake.
But proud they are,
    And tall they stand.
While winds,
    They make them bend and bend.

Marijke

Celtic Castle And Woods 1950-2000

Majestic sun glinting through those careworn walls,
Where once mighty Welsh-born kings marched through noble halls.

Shrouded by the canopy of burnished gold beech
Arms reaching over the babbling brook, its lesson to teach.

Through the seasons, timeless, patient, all excesses do curb,
With changes so subtle as not to disturb.

A child remembering arms laden with bluebells, away from the city,
Banks of deep blue touching the soul for all eternity.

Today, pale imitation, not enough for one hand,
Splashed on green, managed, tamed, patrolled woodland.

No more wild raspberries or cutting a swathe through the wood's
                                                    secret heart.
Torn asunder, tortured, bleeding open, ripped apart.

Paths like dual carriageways, two-wheeled barbarians ~ bring back
                                                    gorse!
Gapped wooden walkways claiming small dogs' paws.

Colossal roped play areas for the human great apes.
More space required for man's favourite toy ~ land knows rapes.

Trolleys dragged to green open spaces where once there were trees,
Another walk ruined, men hunting for balls on their knees.

What is the point?

A secret walled garden, mansion long gone, love makes amends.
Reflect in a quiet place on inscriptions, not to the master but his
                                                    faithful friends!

The soul of the woods endures the present, echoes the past,
And renews for the future as only love ever lasts.

  T M Wright

After The Rain

('. . . in every hour and place visions await the soul . . . ')

Soft, soft, as you walk the land,
footsteps fade in blowing sand.
Hush, hush, do not rush.
Take time to remember every bush.
Listen, let the notes be heard
of each tiny, singing bird.

Water from high, the rain has settled
on leaves of trees and beds of nettles,
where ladybird rests, the fires quenched,
while all about is seeming drenched.
Globular pearls of crystal water
shine like diamond on the hand of daughter.

Oh! Do you not see the rainbow's gleam,
from each clear drop, in endless streams?
As I look down upon wet, leafy park,
upon each cleaned leaf is shining, coloured spark.
Oh wonder! The clothing of trees is such light,
multiple flowers so bright in my sight.

'Didn't you realise?' a friend remarks
then speaking of physics, prisms and quarks.
Strangely, this beauty, before I'd not seen.
Yet to see it again, I still remain keen.
The fragile beauty of angles and light
seen through glass darkly until all is right.

Kristyna Zdrojkowska

Nature All Around

I hear the gurgling of the river,
and the swishing of the trees.
Feel the silence in the forest,
hear the sounds upon the breeze.

I hear the trilling of the Skylark,
while he's soaring way up high.
Down he drops, just like a stone,
then just silence fills the sky.

I see the Swallows, darting past me,
catching insects on the wing,
While avoiding all around them,
their flying is a wondrous thing.

I watch the Blackbird in the garden,
as he scans the ground for worms,
There are hungry mouths to feed,
when he to his young returns.

The forest trees and fields I see,
Dame mother nature at her best.
I see the view, enjoy the scene,
across the land from East to West.

D K Adam

Most Wonderful Thing

The sun gently rises,
Birds softly sing,
Dew on the cobwebs,
Like pearls on a string.

The wildlife is stirring,
Rabbits at play,
Such is the sight,
At the breaking of day.

Flowers slowly open,
Scents fill the air,
A rainbow of colour to be
Seen everywhere.

The sun gently rises,
Birds softly sing,
I think it's God's
Most wonderful thing.

Emmanuel McErlean

The Garden Of Paradise

A huge, brick wall encompassed a wondrous sight,
Never before had I witnessed a garden full of such beauty and
delight.
A palatial haven ~ it took my breath away,
I will forever remember my visit on that scorching summer's day.
For a garden of paradise lay beyond the brick barricade,
Thriving in the sun, and for an eternity I could have stayed.
Roses bloomed in neat little beds,
Hues of yellow, pink and a vivid scarlet red.
Their delicate petals fragile and sheer,
And from their sweet blossom, bees did appear.
Elegant, contoured stems supported them with such poise,
And as I explored this domain, the world seemed exempt from noise.
Lilies, chaste in colour, looked as pure white as freshly fallen snow,
And you could see the fragrant, lilac lupin beginning to grow.
A sea of blue meandered down one side of the plot,
Due to an array of bluebells and pretty forget-me-nots.
Daffodils like blazing sunshine swayed on the breeze,
A myriad of apples and pears adorned the many fruit trees.
Daisies blanketed the fresh, green lawn,
The azure pond had been taken over by the resident frog spawn.
Perched on a willow's gnarled branch were magpies and crows,
Basking in the sun's radiant glows.
An air of serenity was created by cool water flowing,
From a cupid-shaped fountain, which stood proud and knowing.
Every imaginable colour lay before my eyes,
And the deepest sea blue graced the clear skies.
I explored this garden of Eden until the daylight slowly slipped away,
Knowing that I would once again visit this tranquil wonderland some
day.

Emma Smith (17)

Seasons Past

The mocking laughter of the breeze
Amongst the proud yellow corn-tips
Lulls my ceaseless thoughts
Into safe oblivion of the senses

The heady blanket of honeysuckle
Catches my winter-slept nostrils alive
With the tingling simplicity of Spring
And its sharp tang of awakening

My grey-lidded eyes simmer
With the dazzling drops of dew
Hidden amongst the velvety-tips
Of nature's first-born children

As my smile reflects this sight
Joining the hum of the cycle of life
My thoughts spread feelers
Into the dwelling of my being

Contrasted against this poignancy
Encrusted in my soul and hidden
Lies the Spring I choose to Winter
Unwatered, airless, in solitude

Touched by fate, yet without
The calm testing of time
Only the same tune melodiously sung
Cut before the breath escapes

Such Spring lies waiting
Enriched only by meaningless glimpses
Of the cool of the shade
Amongst life's hedgerows and thorns

Waiting only 'if' and 'for'
Without the pull of nature's chosen
Sleepy with the heady yellow blanket
Without fear of the path leading nowhere

For nowhere belongs beneath
And above is only for dreamers
Snug within my mind's own cavern
Lies the chance I have, and have forgotten

Linda Russell

Autumn On Stoneygate

Bronze leaves scrimmage vainly,
desperately defying gusty wind.
Inwardly yearning for the rigid
backbone of a rippling branch.

Battered newspapers whirl impishly,
manoeuvred by unseen threads.
Cheerfully discarding their shackles,
as they revel in gleeful abandon.

Contorted drink cans proliferate,
strewn across a once green verge.
Trampled firmly into earth,
obstinately holding their ground.

Fractured benches stand rejected,
surreally out of place.
Clustered litter piling reverently,
amidst their concrete feet.

Passers-by raise their collars,
studiously ignoring the scene.
Ebony skies quickening footsteps,
as they dream of warmer climes.

Paul Kelly

When Winter Comes

When leaves are changed from green to gold
And north wind blows and bites with cold
Birds on the wing point south to sun
When voles and moles 'neath frost do run
The once rich soil has turned to stone
And Jack Frost nips you to the bone
Then red robin does his hop
Against a snowy white backdrop
The holly bush then it will feed
All God's creatures full of need
And daring mice eat of its fruit
Then run to hide from hunter's hoot
When all hedgehogs have gone to sleep
Dreaming dreams of nights to creep
Where birds lived, while warm we guessed
Now trees bare, reveal the nest
Dark are the nights with winter's veil
And sun-tanned skins begin to pale
The shortest day and longest night
From this point hence, eves gain more light
All children's glee at falling white
On with their boots and out they fight
Treads crack their imprints in the snow
Cheeks rosy red with inner glow
On lakes' ice mantel geese will glide
And foxes catch 'twixt cubs divide
When winter comes, that is when
I'm in my loved ones again.

Gary W Allen

Outside

Slanted Sunday sunlight falling through the air,
Sunshine shining, forming slats of light in the early morning glare,
Gushing waves upon the sandy bed,
Plants blowing in the wind on the beachy head,
The undulating dunes of grainy sand,
The picturesque landscape of the coastal land,
The reflective surface of the calm rippling pool,
The twisting turning tides, shimmering and cool,
The gliding insects and butterflies, floating in the heather,
Blustering, flowing, falling in the ether,
The immovable blanket of sludgy slime,
Immovable quicksand, jump back in time,
Towering cliffs of glittering sapphire,
The insatiable sun, a ball of fire,
Doves, gulls and sealife endure,
Unconquerable cliffs, sturdy and sure,
Off to the east as the crow flies,
On the far side of the ocean, into the sunrise.

Julie Ann Evans

Bitter About Litter

Why, oh why, in the great outdoors,
    Do many humans leave their marks,
By dropping litter on the floors
    Of beauty spots? It really narks
Me when I see
    This demonstration of stupidity.

A little thought, consideration,
    Would alleviate the situation;
Checking in front, around, behind them,
    Leaving scenes just as they find them,
Leaving only the rural features,
    Ensuring the safety of feral creatures.

When every human is educated,
    The scenery decontaminated,
Perhaps all beings will enjoy
    The countryside; not to destroy
But to enhance
    And give the natural world a chance.

Gordon Cuthbert

River To Nowhere

Come with me
To the water's edge.
You can see the ducks
And geese waiting for their daily feed ~
They are so free.

Look at the fish swimming,
Like dancers they glide
Across the water.
Making ripples behind them
Waiting for the next ride.

Watch the yachtsmen having a race.
They calculate and observe moves ~
Going faster to reach the end.
Water spraying everywhere.
Only one can win ~
But on the mind
It can depend.

Wait for the sun
To reflect the days' end.
Going over what you can see
Slowly fading away
Into the stillness
Until another day . . .

Jagdeesh Sokhal

Winter Animals

White snow brushes across the air and land.
People lend a sore, red and battered hand.
No more green leaves or buds on trees, but pale brown frosted
                                                        branches.
Little mice hide away, cuddled up warm, they don't take any chances.

Fog rising over the hillside, so high.
A tiny bird attempts to fly.
A thin dog looks at you with lonely eyes.
In a burrow a cold rabbit lies.

Robin glances across the White.
A small cold sun gives off a ribbon of light.
The landscape bare, torn and white.
Wolves curl up for a long cold night.

Craig Hall (11)

Walking Back To Happiness

I was so sad and lonely,
My husband died you see,
The children all had fled the nest,
That meant there was only me.
I didn't know which way to turn,
Until one day I saw,
A poster about rambles,
Pinned upon a door.
I plucked up courage and went along,
A five-mile walk to do.
I met some lovely people,
And made some good friends too.
Since then my life has been just great,
I love the hills and dales.
The rivers and the waterfalls,
The sunshine and the gales.
To walk in any season,
Be it rain or snow,
Gives one a happy feeling,
And a really healthy glow.
So if you're feeling on your own,
You too should go along,
And join in with the ramblers,
You simply can't go wrong.

P Dargan

All Alone

The great outdoors it beckons to me
In the fresh air I can feel so free
Blue sky above and sun on my face
    as I wander alone at a steady pace

To feel the wind blowing through my hair
To walk the hills without a care
Leaving the filthy city behind
    and the flotsam and jetsam of mankind

I climb, I walk, alone I trudge
As my poor husband will not budge
A 'couch potato' that's not me
    I know the name of every tree

I stride along in my hiking boots
Looking for the easier routes
But now it's time to rest my feet
    and enjoy the food I brought to eat

I pass several others enjoying their walk
Some are silent ~ and some will talk
I'm happy to be here on my own
    far away from the mobile phone

But now the sun is beginning to fade
I sit for a moment in dappled shade
Now I must leave this place so pretty
    back to my home in the grimy city

    M Scott

Nature

The grass is green,
the sky is blue,
and the flowers bloom
in front of you.

The flowers are red,
yellow and pink.
The leaves are green
as you have seen.

Lynette Thistlethwaite (11)

Kelstern

*(Two miles from the village, high on the Wolds, North West of Louth.
Opened 1943. Closed 1945)*

Naked lies a warriored soil and forgotten where, the Station Gate.
But keenly lies this heroed toil and listens now the whispering wait
As slowly up the Ludford road a Ludensian makes a sinner's climb
Whose memories are open code that call again a Bomber's time

For in these bedded Lincoln hills, Hanover is never, yet forgot
Though dispersal pan is turnip drilled and won, the fight he fought
Smells an ancient newly country smell, of a land that's set aside
And pilgrim tolls a passing bell for years of unadmitting pride

The field is past and future now, for Kelstern, lingers, in its bed
As comes the whispering hour to bow, a nightly converse with its
dead
And some may talk and some may hate and many watch out for the
flare
That lifting bravely sinful weight, a promise, to fly the angel air

Awaiting still the briefing call to go, one last, remembered trip
Begins a velvet murmuring glow, that signals duty's crypt
Comes holy words of yonder ken, on lips from gathered time
As ages wearied, aircrewmen, speak an ancient faeried rhyme

For Brooke has only Granchester, and Coleridge, Xanadu
But Lincoln has a Lancaster and Coningsby makes two
And six and twenty-five set in Kelstern's sacred stones,
Keep safely as they strive, to watch the consecrated bones.

So closely holds this secret of a sorrowed, country yield
That comes only to the pallid, who can whisper in the field.
For Ludensis hears the Bomber where poets listen for the wind
And silence is misnomer, stiffly homaged for the sinned.

Francis McDermott

27

Autumn

I love the autumn season
With all its different hues
It's as if nature has decided
To let us revel in her news,
That with winter fast approaching
Beware of the winter blues!

Remember her coat of many colours
Reds, orange, browns and gold
As together leaves mix and mingle
A wondrous sight to behold.
Like mischievous sprites, they dip and dance
Unaware of the coming cold.

As each little gust of wind
Lifts the autumn leaves on high,
Swooping . . . ever upwards
Swirling furiously ~ they fly.
The richness of their many colours
Standing out against the sky!

As nature's coat begins to fall
Look closely on the ground.
Beneath the trees, their branches bare
There is beauty to be found.
As the winds abate, in the cold night air
See leaves, gathered all around.

Under this coat of many colours
Hedgehogs now play hide and seek
They have found a cosy bed,
In which to go to sleep,
To hibernate, for winter
Whilst the snow lies thick and deep.

I adore the autumn season
With her colours rich and bold
As the wind whips leaves into a frenzy
I forget about the cold
I can only watch in awe and wonder
As nature's miracles unfold.

Gwyneth Wynn-Davies

Spring

New life, very bright mornings,
Love in the air,
Yellow heads dance with joy,
Beauty buds open with light green magic.

Swallows return,
Your flight of wonder,
Bluebell woods of charm,
Sunshine clarity.

John Reddish

Beachcomber

Pearls of stone
on sandy beaches
there for the world to see

Garlands
of Sea Weed
Garlands galore
on the shore . . . and there's more

Shells and shells
    and
bits of wood
       footprints
where my Lady stood
    all
to be swallowed
by the tide ~
      to return
      and return
      and return.

Dave Iredale

Untitled

O nature in your hour of need, man turns his head,
Ignores your cry. We fell the forest, pollute land and
Sea, now look to space, more harm to do. If only we
Could be content, with what the earth has offered.
Let's stop this race for outer space, and concentrate
On Mother Earth.

We walk the forests' shaded paths, from hilltops high,
Admire the view, so when we leave, please don't forget,
You brought your litter, so take it back.

Denis Paton

Tall Trees In The Garden

I am very fond of the small spinney
at the bottom of my garden.

It started with a formation of six
different species. Saplings planted
27 years ago.

A Birch, Weeping Willow, Laburnum,
Mountain Ash, Sycamore and Conifer.
I added a Flowering Cherry and made
it the centrepiece. Pleasing to look at.

All have skyrocketed much to the annoyance
of my neighbour. She had the gall to call
them a cemetery collection. In her sharp words they
needed cutting back. She said they cut out their light.

Trees to me are God-given. Majestic and
haughty like sentinels. They never cloud my day.
In Spring they are a shelter for the defiant song
of a pair of blackbirds.

Sacrilege to uproot and turn into timber for the
kitchen AGA.

J F Jenkins

The Country Footpath

The country footpath is, for me, a faithful friend
Which leads me, day-by-day, where I would go
On many wondrous journeys, and turning many bends
To satisfy my varied wanderings to and fro.

It meanders, ever upwards, to the nearby hills
To places where, as yet, it seems few have been,
It helps us leave behind all worries and all ills,
Presenting every walker with a wholesome scene.

The changing hedgerows are its friends, and mine,
Like silent sentries, standing ever faithful by its side,
Where fragrant wild rose and the busy eglantine
Present that rural beauty which nought can ever hide.

It leads us through the many coloured farming fields
Just like a patchwork quilt upon a well-made bed,
Where varied root-crops, wheat, and cabbages it yields,
For former country folk by these were then mostly fed.

Here tread the hooves of horse and sometimes cow
Animals forming such a part of rural farming scene,
And folk who walked from church on balmy evenings, somehow
Choosing to wander here where most former faithful folk had been.

This footpath leads me o'er the many gentle slopes
Which, in some places, beckon to West Lancashire's rich plain,
And somehow seem to merge where the distant hillside gropes,
The place where journeys end and we must homewards turn again.

Then when at last this journey mine is clearly done,
And when my last stile I will finally have clambered o'er,
This path I love just now will lead back to the setting sun
Where tomorrow's daylight can promise me much more.

Bill Guy

The Gift Of Life

The Thundering Rivers and the Raging Seas are nothing but water,
The Mountainous Mountains and the miles of Land are nothing but
                                                            soil,
But we who live in this world of land and sea,
Are gifted with life that we share with everyone and everything
                                                    around us.

Danielle Williams (11)

Autumn

Autumn, another season
Flowers fading, petals falling
Squirrels darting from trees to ground
Gathering nuts, so quick and agile
Newly ploughed fields, deep with furrows
Stretching forever, shades of brown
Leaves swirl silently, a golden carpet
Mingled with yellows, as grass dies down
A carpet of nature, one encounters
God made them all, this beauty around

Elizabeth Troth

Soul Walk

Standing on the edge,
breeze of summer's passion
blows through me,

heat of day becomes
night of ecstasy,
swimming naked,

your touch, searing
like the summer sun,
burns my skin.

Day or night,
summer's passions,
take a walk over
my soul.

Angela Peters

The 'Concreting' Earth

When Earth was blue and green,
Many, many aeons ago
Beauty, Harmony and Freedom
Reign the lands of this humble orb.
But now that man has become the lord
He is hell-bent on replacing Nature's work.

Once where there were trees and rivers,
Now there are light-poles and roads;
Once where there were greens and foliages
Now there are concretes and buildings;

Once where there were camels, horses and carts,
Now there are cars, trains and lorries.
Once where there were clean, fragrance 'airs',
Now there are dirty, chemicalised shrouds.

> Power, as with any entity
> Succumbs the entity
> To show its true nature.

Mahesh Patel

Thoughts Of Spring

The fragrant air is gentle once again,
There is a freshness in the soft rain,
Blossoms quiver and open in pink and white,
The warm sun caresses in its bright light.

Clusters of daffodils are in golden flower,
Sparkling with drops from a fleeting shower,
And tulips in vivid hues, straight and proud,
Now forgotten the gloom of winter's shroud.

Once again life has a wonderful zest,
As everything stirs after the long rest,
Nature's magic wand touches the land,
Lovers happily wander hand in hand.

Blackbirds and thrushes sing sweetly again,
Such beauty cannot fail to soften pain,
Harshly felt in bleak days now gone by,
In glorious spring it's tears of joy we cry!

Joan Miles

Camping

Let's go camping, the great outdoors
I bet it rains, I bet it pours
I set up camp and then I see
A cheeky squirrel watching me

I settle down as night draws near
Wondering what sounds I'll hear
There's an owl hooting loud
I imagine him wise and proud

The birds start to sing as dawn breaks
Such songs could cure the worst heartaches
And there's a hedgehog dashing by
Past the burrows rabbits occupy

At the river a fox quenches its thirst
But I think a young deer got there first
I see her running into the trees
How I love mornings like these

So I'm glad I went camping out in the wild
It didn't rain and it stayed quite mild
To wake up to nature is such a pleasure
It's one of those times that I will treasure

Ann Thornton

Sunflower

A blaze of yellow,
Shimmering, shining in the sun,
Now hard to imagine the seed
Where you begun.

Your head tilted down,
Leaves the size of hands,
Face of golden brown,
At six feet tall you stand,
Majestic mother nature has
Made you simply grand!

Lynne M Brown

The Walk

The call it comes to one and all,
Whether you be short or tall,
Fat or thin, young or old,
It casts a spell or so I'm told.

Whether it be wet or dry
You know you must go out and try,
The sun might shine and make you sizzle
Or clouds drift o'er and on you drizzle.

What magic is it drives you forth?
If you come from South or North
Or East or West it's all the same,
To take part, yes that's the aim.

Where e'er you live the choice is yours,
Perhaps balmy air along the shores,
A breezy trek across the dale
Or sheltered in a nearby vale.

You breathe in deep the glorious air,
Perfumes rich are always there,
Beauteous views are there to see,
Are you in heaven? You well could be.

Yes it's lovely and what's more
Nature holds an open door,
So step outside it's there for free
A wondrous gift for you and me.

Peter D G Bird

Our Green And Pleasant Land

Cherish our countryside,
Follow rules and codes.
Shut gates behind you,
Don't step on toads.
Take litter home,
Don't pollute our fields.
It's harmful to wildlife,
And affects the milk yields.
Look and admire,
At the crops and the grain.
Don't trample the harvest,
It won't grow again!
Breathe in the clean air,
Don't contaminate it with fumes.
Leave the car on the road,
And step in between the blooms.
If we cherish our countryside,
And stand proud as a nation,
We can preserve our heritage,
For the coming generation.

Sally Jobson

Man Keeps Trying

Higher than the birds fly man perches
Like an Eagle high on the edge of a mountain.
He pauses spider-like in his web of ropes
To gaze around, and feel completely
Insignificant against the splendour of the world
Spread out around him.
Its beauty, its power, and its creativity
Can only humble he who for a short time
Shares in Nature's privacy.
But with caution man also must assess
For swift as the seconds that tick on by
Nature can become restless, and as if angry
At man's intrusion, withdraws her kind hand
Offering instead her icy kiss.
And storms to loosen man's tentative grip.
The mountain does not side against Nature's call
But joins the game to cause man's fall.
Yet, over and over, man will return to
Face the mountains and fickle Nature
And try to win them over.

Olga Johnson

Summer Afternoon

Wild rose, vetch and honeysuckle
    entangle in the hedge.
Green tree-shadow, twisted root by reedbed,
    quiver at water's edge.

A few fishermen sit waiting
    for hidden prey to bite
but ~ sudden flash of green and blue ~
    then, tantalising sight
as a Kingfisher flies away
    with the Fish of their Dream.
They watch till ripples cease to spread
    in a cloud-silvered stream
and, perhaps, one philosopher
    thinks it just like *his* life:
whenever wish-fulfilment near
    a snag, problem ~ or strife.

A dragonfly with glinting wing
    flies to where steps ascend,
past a butterfly fluttering
    as though life had no end
to where the bridge cast deep shadow
    and puddles have not dried.
Stray people find it chilly there
    unlike the swans that glide
on through tunnel to summer day,
    past each water meadow,
familiar sight, scent, colour,
    spied on by fish below.

Willow trees watch, know who is who.
But that's what all things conscious do.

    C M Creedon

God's Wonderful World

To see the dawn of a brand New Day,
The Wonder of coming light,
To see so many things appear
From out the dark of night.

The Summit of a mountain,
The Grandeur of its Height,
The golden beams of sunlight
Fills one with great delight.

The little gentle hills appear,
How Picturesque are they,
Their lovely little rolling hills,
Appear at break of day.

How soon we hear the bird song,
What nicer sound at Dawn,
To fill our hearts with gladness
And start a brand new Morn.

So many wonders round us,
For us to see each day,
The trees all blowing in the breeze,
And lovely flowers in May.

And then the snow in Winter,
A wonder of delight,
The miracle of seasons
Fills one with sheer delight.

Just pause and watch and listen,
As you pass on your way,
The Wonders of the Lord appear
More and more each passing day.

A Kendall

The Great Outdoors

Green fields and open spaces we do like
Rambling over hills and dales enjoying a day's hike
Sunny skies and a ride on a bike
Followed by a dip in the dike.

Nature is such a wonderful thing
Watching birds build their nests and listening to them sing
Bulbs popping up their heads saying is it spring.
Church bells tolling their familiar ring.

Camp fires burn as night draws on
Sleeping outdoors is so much fun
Waking up to the birds calls and sun
The great outdoors is enjoyed by everyone.

L J Male

AM Lower Hillside

Through border land October hues
carpet in star-spangled manner,
to vacuum the pulse of the woodland.

Pigeons unwrap, like a cellophane gift
their wisp of smoke from the fields,
sunlight sprinkling golden dust

on past loves sunk into beech.
But shadows form upon the clouds to carve
implausible dusk, a malice felt

within the root that bleeds the burn to stagnant:
death cap thrives, a murder of crow
fouling the air with their accent,

clutching briar and skeleton fern
at the heart of a barked consensus;
whispers, from pungent hope the rain holds.

D W Gray

Untitled

Clear the seas
Oh don't pollute please
DoN't cut down trees
So you can build factories
Animals arE getting killed
Just foR a little thrill
Pollution is Very high
And I wonder why?
The Earth puTs up with this
So I think it's time
That Our pollution stops
Now!

Jamie Campbell (11)

Nature

The countryside is calling, can't you hear the gentle sound?
Inviting us to see and hear the wonders all around
When spring wakes up the sleeping earth and buds burst everywhere
All nature's beauties are revealed, a sight for all to share

A time of birth for baby lambs and other growing things
Of fur and hoof and tiny paws and also fragile wings
In summer, when the flower show their blooms of every hue
Oh happy carefree halcyon days, beneath the skies of blue

Autumn has its special charm, though days are growing cold
Such glowing colours on the trees, the russet, red and gold
Winter, now a time of rest for nature's growing world
'Neath blanket snow, so crisp and white, such magic is unfurled

We're privileged to share this world, with creatures, plants and trees
So we should treat it with respect, and treasure land and seas

E MacKenzie

Seasons Inside-Outside

Winter is the season's jail
No fragrant blooms and leafless trees
Where man stays in to avoid the breeze
Even the plants stay indoors
Under the wraps of the earthly floor

Next is Spring, a breath of life
New blooms and leaves shine in delight
Birds sing happy, sweet love songs
And build their homes with much aplomb

Bright comes Summer, this is out
Blooms in gardens, lawns cut neat
Farmers happy with the wheat
New fledglings and migrant birds
Fill our senses with sight and words

Finally Autumn completes them all
When many autumn leaves do fall
Hues of reds and shades of gold
Plans for Winter now unfold
Squirrels harvest and make a store
With Winter knocking on the door

Elizabeth Bennett

Lickey Woods

Spring in Lickey Woods
Where we wandered still full of Winter's sleep
And awoke like the trees far beyond the tide line
Our feet washed by an azure sea
Bluebells surging in sheltered groves
Cascading down leaf-strewn banks
Filling every glade
Sad with the colour of Summer skies
Deeper than day before dusk and dawn
Bursting with the scent of lost Summers
And the urgent beauty of a love that cannot last.

Peter P H Dodd

The Blackbird

Is he singing just for me?
Surely not just for me?
Yet I am alone
Only my dog, Ben, as witness.
I look around
No one in sight
The song goes on
Then I see him
A blackbird.
Perched high in the branches of a hawthorn tree
Silhouetted against the pale morning sky,
Shining black,
Bathed in sunlight;
I stand transfixed in the cool
Of the early morning,
My very being filled with rapture
At the beauty of that melody;
Is he singing just for me?
Surely not just for me?
But there is on one else around
To hear that song so beautiful
And I know it was for me.

C Jepson

Blackstone Edge ~ A Pennine View By Night

Northern lights, like a bowl of
Precious gems, amber, red and gold.

Shimmer and shine in the nightime
Streets, swirl and sway in the
Cool night breeze.

Over the moors in the blackness
Ghostly shadows dance,
Spectres prowl in the heather
Waiting for their chance.

Waterfall of raindrops tumble,
In fear entranced you stumble,
Blackstone beckons you over
The edge.

Beverley Anne Eaton-Daley

The Meaning Of The Countryside

To walk through the fields
On an endless summer's day
To sit and watch the farmer
Whilst he's busy making hay.

To walk on through the meadow
And find a leafy glade
To lay down and dream a while
In the coolness of the shade.

To take the time to understand
That this is what it means
To see a canvas made by God
For nature to paint her scenes.

The world would be a lesser place
Without the countryside to hand
So let us learn to keep it safe
And to cherish the glorious land.

Andrew J Pritchard

Four Seasons

Summer sun, shining bright,
Eagles waiting for their winter flight.
Shining buttercups gleaming yellow,
Winter sky clouding summer.

Freezing cold, snowy drifts,
Rain dripping from the sky.
Snowmen made up to six foot high.

Autumn's near, coloured leaves,
Falling from the old dead trees.
Sharp prickly conkers brown,
Tumbling to the muddy ground.

Spring appearing from nowhere,
As if it had no care.
Wild flowers growing from the green, green grass,
Lakes with rippling waters,
All four seasons beautifully pass.

Amy Massey (14)

The Bee

When I was sailing on the sea,
I met a very peculiar bee.
Apparently he was from France,
He started doing a groovy dance
He told me over in the hive,
It was the hippest type of jive.
He showed me his pointy little sting,
(A very useful little thing!)
He shoved it in my finger *ouch!*
Poison pumping from the honeybee's pouch.
Venom flowing from the stinger,
Into my very painful finger!
Then the bee brushed back its antennae,
It was no longer quite so sly,
Because the forsaken little fly had realised
You sting, you die!
The honeybee's flower power
Had suddenly become quite sour.
The little bug a fighter fallen,
Will be collecting no more pollen.

Reuben Quinn (10)

Nature's Gifts
(A Villanelle)

My soul rejoices in such things as these.
The scent of blossoms heavy on the bough.
They soothe the heart and give the spirit ease.

A golden sunset filtering through trees,
The sky at night, the Great Bear and the Plough.
My soul rejoices in such things as these.

Wild rivers rushing onward to the seas,
Passing through meadow, home of sheep and cow.
They soothe the heart and give the spirit ease.

A solitary walk beneath the trees
Where grows the primrose at its finest now.
My soul rejoices in such things as these.

The eagle's grace. Who knows what sights he sees?
A flock of seagulls following the plough.
They soothe the heart and give the spirit ease.

The constant surging of the endless seas,
Each ebb and flow. I almost hear it now.
My soul rejoices in such things as these.
They soothe the heart and give the spirit ease.

Pamela Mann

Seasons In Harmony

The *trumpet* heralds the celebration of *spring*
Its clear long notes signal the birth of new creation. We think of fresh
colours ~ of blue and green, reminding us of youth ~ straight and
tall ~ of joyous laughter and of pain. It is a time of sowing and a time
of learning. Reflect on the daffodils dancing in the breeze. Open your
eyes ~ take hold of life ~ for it is precious and brief.

The *drum* announces the *summer*
Bold ~ vibrant ~ full of expectancy, colour and noise! Listen to the
musical symphony ~ it is the sound of the sea, crashing against the
rocks, with the seagulls crying and wheeling overhead. It is a time of
blessing ~ of dragonflies on rainbow wings, heady perfumed roses, of
beautiful transcending sunsets, giving glory to God their Maker.

The *bagpipes* salute the *autumn's glow*
With mournful and eerie sounds ~ yet rich and gripping to the soul,
bringing tides of nostalgia and melancholia. A time to take stock ~ of
bountiful harvest. The hedgehog snuffles among the leaves, looking
for a safe haven to sleep through the long chilly days to come. The
twittering swallows congregate overhead, ready to depart to warmer
climes. A time of peace and tranquillity ~ of prayer and thanksgiving.

The mellow tones of the *cello* pay homage to *winter's* call
Reflection ~ experience and wisdom ~ like vintage wine. It is a time
of pastel shades ~ of growing old ~ of replenishing by sleep. A
solitary blackbird proclaims the serenity of evensong, as darkness'
cloak falls. The advent candle hails approaching new life ~ all is well!
The circle complete ~ and it all begins once more.

Yvonne August

The Forest Dawn

The chimney smoke drifts slowly, above the trees so tall,
Which marks the spot of the woodman's cot, by a waterfall.
He rises as the dawn sleeps on, his family aren't forsaken.
He'll be gone, part of the morn, and return when they awaken.

'Jack', the black retriever, greets him warmly ~ no surprise,
For this excitement and elation, is found only at sunrise.
This time of day is special, to old faithful and his master,
Both know the fun, of the twin-barrelled gun, and the game
'Jack' chases after.

Into the dark unknown they stride, the night-life still enhances,
Stealthily stalking from tree to tree, while roe deer continue their
                                                              prances.
Weasels still dance their frolicking jigs, and squirrels leap to and fro,
Leverets practise their highest jump ever, over a grazing doe.

The pheasant and the partridge, go courting two by two,
Woodcock and wild turkey, alas, they'll end up dinner stew.
Adder and the wise owl, keep an eye on everyone,
Whilst foxy and the badger, exercise at a run.

The falcon and the sparrow hawk, hover in the wind,
Field mouse helps Mr Mole, to find his next-of-kin.
The otter and the wild duck, swim across the shallow stream,
Wild pig chases hazel grouse, in the relay team.

But forest play then disappears, on the woodman's noisy arrival,
They run here, there, everywhere, only thinking of survival.
And so back home the hunters go, with rabbit, bird and fawn,
I don't pretend, my furry friends . . .
Take care at the 'forest dawn'.

Alistair J H Watson

Oil Spillage

Who did it, who spilt the oil?
Who did such a shameful thing?
Was it a tanker, was it a pipe?
Nobody knows how it happens.
Was it done on purpose,
or was it not?
How many birds has it turned black;
how many beaches has it spoiled.
How many people go to the beach now?
Who is the evil one?
Who is the innocent one?
Boats are trying to mop it up,
but still it slimes like a snake,
it's still travelling round the world.
Who spilt the oil?

Greg Hardy (9)

The Beauty Of Nature

When Springtime appears, with nature's array
The buds shooting forth, bringing flowers to display
The birds singing high, in the trees up above
Like a glorious feeling of forthcoming love.

Look for the beauty, it's there all around
Just waiting, enchanting, so easily found
God made this for us, to savour with delight
So keeping watching, enjoying, all of nature in sight.

Although Springtime will pass, Summertime will replace
The day much longer, sunny days showing face
Always look on the bright side, keep smiling, it's fun
The sunshine of nature is a prize to be won.

When Summertime has gone past, then Autumn appears
The nature bells ringing, with their message of cheers
The leaves on the trees, are a joy to behold
With their masses of colours, like medals of gold.

The passing of Autumn, Wintertime has begun
The shortening of days, with the lowering of sun
But look up for the sunshine, of nature from above
God shines upon us, with his mighty love.

Williamina Gibb

Highland Dawn

From the depth of the forest green glinting gold
Shimmering rays of sunshine so bold
Silently treading eyes watchful and clear
At the edge of the forest they prance in their fear

Fields rich with colour tease them and call
Birds singing softly bluebells tinkling, cajole
Wild flowers dancing seductively sway to the
Beautiful dawn of a new summer day

Slowly emerging stance regal and proud
The morning sun rising surrounds them in gold
Fawns herded together safe in their midst
To the eye a chimera shrouded in mist

This memory I treasure fills me with awe
Eyes disbelieving the wonder I saw
Nature at dawn, deer grazing near
Colours unreal yet vivid and clear

The most beautiful time of the year is this
Nature has given her wonderful gift
No matter the highlands or lowlands you be
A walk in our country is something to see

Mary O'Hara

Contentment

I love the end of day
When the evening falls,
And the resting sun
Skims the rim of the hill,
Sending grey shadows
To meet the gentle dusk.

The miles are ended and
The contours climbed;
Only the leaf-mould now,
Soft on the kindly path.
Ahead, beyond the turn,
Voices drift on the air.
All is contentment.

And if, at the end of day,
The distance covered and
The challenge of the climb
Discharged with honour,
I plot a gentle path
Among the psalmist's hills,
The sunlight beckoning
Beyond the shadows,
I shall go home content.

Glenda A White

Woodland Wonders

It's quiet here on this woodland path
At least it looks that way
But what if we should stop a while
To watch the creatures play.

A rustling way up in the tree
Causes leaves to fall
As Sammy Squirrel flies overhead
He's playing there that's all.

Well Sammy has disturbed someone
We hear Fred Pheasant's cries
A twig then snaps and interest shows
In Baby Bambi's eyes.

What has she seen that interests her
In the leaves that move about?
Bambi jumps as out of them
Appears old Hedgehog's snout.

So next time you are in the woods
Tread softly whilst you roam
Or you might find that you've destroyed
Old Willie Weasel's home!

Close gates and leave no litter
Never light a fire in here
Allow our precious wildlife
To live safely ~ not in fear.

Shirley-Anne Cruickshank

In The Garden

I sit in the garden, and admire the view,
And watch as the butterflies,
And bees look for honey.
The wallflowers strong and sturdy,
Are we now their hope and glory?
While the butterflies you see,
Favour the flower of the Sweet Pea.
The gladioli are just budding,
By September they will be humming,
With the bees in their season,
Making honey, that's their reason.

Thru the cabbage and sprout patch,
The caterpillars they can munch.
With the beetles eating the tatties,
And the carrots get a crunch.
The cauli's with their white appeal,
Brings the greenfly into use.
I wait there patiently, spray in hand,
So that I can keep them off my land.
When the sunset begins to fall,
The heavens open, the rain does fall.

Little titbits of bread, nuts and all,
On the bird table for the birds do call.
There's all types that come, both big and small,
Come to the garden and sit on the wall.
There's seagulls, blackbirds, crows and jays,
Who grab at the food with no delay.
They scare off the little 'uns when on the roof,
I realise this mistake I have to improve.

There's wrens, finches, sparrows and blue-tits,
Who pick at the crumbs, nuts and bacon bits.
But inside the bird house there's a big feast,
Just so the little 'uns can have a treat.
There's martins and robins during the closing season,
Nesting in boxes and that's a good reason.
They cling to the strips of fatty bacon,
During the spring and autumn season.

The Instant Song Man

Summer Reverie

How we long for summer to arrive,
To feel again it's good to be alive.
Lighter nights, warmer days and cheery sun
All promise a new era has begun.

The gentle caress of a cooling breeze
With not enough knots to disturb the trees
Is a welcome event on a hot summer's night
As you sip a long cool drink in the fading light.

Basking in the sun or wisely in the shade,
Drowsily enjoying a lark's serenade.
A neighbour's barbecue adding flavour to the summer air,
Moistening your palate at the thought of a steak medium rare.

Lolling on the lawn with your body mostly bare,
Achieving an all-over tan that will make people stare.
Your skin shining with the oil that will protect
For a while from the danger of the sun rays direct.

Your hopes are often high that life is for pleasure
During this uplifting season made for leisure.
Take every chance of enjoying the weather when kind,
As we all know autumn is not far behind.

Allen Jessop

Apple Blossoms

In awe I stand and stare.
But could it simply be at
the force of life, which
runs through branches
bent by heavy blossoms?
Or could it simply be
feeling their joy jingle
my heart, now feasting in
forgotten fairy lands?
My eyes fulfil the mind
which then moves deeper,
reaching down inside.

And from my roots within
love's spreading forth
to your roots, tree.

Daniela Lampariello Taylor

The Blackbirds

I fly down to the corner of the yard each day
Where stands a dish of water clean and clear
In which I bathe to my heart's content
And without the slightest sense of fear.

For the owners of this yard and dish I know
To blackbirds are always thoughtful and kind
Putting nuts and seeds out in the winter time
When our normal food is hard to find.

When the winter months are passed and gone
And spring puts on her vernal dress,
That's when my other half starts hunting round
For the place to build her nest.

Having laid her eggs and brooding now
It's a placid time for her each day,
But she still comes to have her bath
While I perch up high and sing away.

The sparrows also come to our bathing dish,
For them it's merely to take a drink
And we don't mind them doing this,
They're really only sitting on the brink.

In a short while now I'll have lots to do
Finding food for my young chicks,
Also teaching them what they need to know,
How to survive and knowing all the tricks.

Such as avoiding pussy cats galore
Who lay in wait for their chance
To spring at us poor blackbirds
When they think it's time to pounce.

In the meantime though I'll take another bath
Seeing as the water has been changed today,
And maybe teach my young ones too,
How to bathe in the blackbird's happy way.

Gerard Oxley

Silent Wings

They came on Silent Wings ~
Suddenly, shimmering
In the Summer light ~
A multicoloured rainbow ~
Like stained glass
Glittering in the sunshine ~
Peacock, Tortoiseshell, Emperor ~
Beautiful butterflies
Dancing on a garden stage.

A sudden breeze
And swiftly they were gone ~
On Silent Wings,
In the twinkling of an eye.
An empty sky,
Now clouded over ~
Where is the Swallowtail,
Brimstone, Orange-Tip?
Beautiful butterflies farewell ~
Dance again when sunshine comes!

Elizabeth Egerton

Me And Jodie

Me and Jodie by the pool
two little people trying
        to be cool,

Running water in the back
-ground, soothing sound to
        our ears,
I hope that life will be
    kind to her!

Me and Jodie by the pool
summer sun bright and hot
we just sit and talk a lot
little birds come to feed
we just watch them take
        what they need,
    Hawfinch, Greenfinch
        Sparrows too
Blackbirds singing from the
        trees.

Me and Jodie by the pool
it's so very obvious that
life's a school, forever
learning every day all
life's lessons that come
        our way!

Me and Jodie by the pool
two little people being
        cool,
what you gave me money
couldn't buy, that
wonderful time made
Papa feel so high!

Dylan Thomas Jones

Seasons

Springtime spreads a carpet,
 Of Yellow, White and Blue.
With Crocuses and Daffodils,
 And the dainty Snowdrop too.

The Primrose and the Bluebells,
 That bloom throughout the Spring.
Beneath a leafy canopy,
 Where a host of songbirds sing.

In May we hear the Cuckoo,
 All day we hear him call.
And trees burst into blossom,
 All too soon, their petals fall.

The busy Bees and Butterflies,
 They dance amongst the flowers.
Collecting pollen and nectar,
 Between the Summer's showers.

The perfume from the Roses,
 The smell of new-mown hay,
That drifts across the meadow,
 At the end of a Summer's day.

The fields of corn that turn to Gold,
 As Autumn it draws near,
And faded flowers shed their seeds,
 To bloom again next year.

Autumn brings her colours,
 To the hedgerows and the trees,
As falling leaves, and morning mists,
 Drift gently on the breeze.

Soon Autumn turns to Winter,
    With Frost, and Snow and Rain,
But I know it won't be long,
    Till Springtime's here again.

Brian Saunders

Outdoors: All Year Round

Come for a walk in the bracing spring
Violets and daffodils bloom
Birds nests a-making
Hedgehogs awaking
Breezes chase off the gloom.

Saunter through summer's meadows green
Under the golden sun
Roses in bloom
Holidays loom
Time to relax and have fun.

Kick around copper, russet and red
Of autumn's leaves a-dying
Harvests of corn
Mists in the morn
While swallows south are flying.

Crunch winter's frost beneath your feet
See trees all draped in white
Holly berries out
Robins about
Christmas, and then Twelfth Night!

Elsie M Karbacz

A Walk In The Park

A walk in the park in morn's early haze
The splendour of nature, her beauty ablaze
My hour of quiet life's worries can wait
As I follow the pathway inside the gate.

There is always a welcome, the flowers, the bees
A column of birches sway light in the breeze
Whilst a sturdy old oak that stands nearby
Throws out its branches to reach to the sky.

I cannot but wonder at tales it could tell
Of lovers who paused at the old wishing well
A kiss that was stolen, entwining of hands
It knows of them all from the spot where it stands.

Laughter of children, many secrets to tell
Plopping of pebbles as they pass by the well
Never a worry, never a care
Skipping along in the clear morning air.

Scarlet robed poppies laze in the sun
Nodding their heads to greet everyone
High in the Heavens sweet sound of a lark
The air steeped in magic as I walk in the park.

A rainbow of colour from the rose in her bed
At first call of the sunshine she raises her head
Proud in her glory, welcomes morning anew
Petals of velvet, teardrops of dew.

As the roar of a lion the world cannot wait
Hustle and bustle outside the gate
But here in this haven with the song of the lark
Peace reigns in abundance on my walk in the park.

Barbara Davies

The Blackbird

Little blackbird, every day
You dance upon my balcony
I'm sure I know what you seek
With your brilliant orange beak
I only muster breaded crumbs
Then the greedy pigeon comes
And completely rules the stage
This fills my head and heart with rage

The blackbird though, is unperturbed
Indifferent to the larger bird
He gracefully erects its tail
And hops upon the joining rail
To sing a song, for me alone
Blotting out the pigeon's drone

This thing of beauty, not just for me
But for all the world to hear and see

Roland Seager

Where Roses Grow

(In memory of Great Aunt Emmy whose countryside, for 96 years, was a small garden in South Hackney, East London)

In London town the roses grow
    Across the way at Kew,
You'll find them not on Shepherd's Bush
    Nor down by Waterloo,
But in the East at Bethnal Green
    Or down the Mile End Road,
You'll find upon the market stalls,
    Sweet roses, tied and bowed ~

They come up from the countryside,
    All fresh upon a train
With fruit and veg and monkey nuts,
    And cockles for Brick Lane.
There are roses white and roses red
    And some in shades of blue ~
While some are sold as Valentines,
    Kissed with morning dew.

Though many, many years ago,
    A lady in a fret,
Did throw a rose, yes, Billy's rose,
    To Nellie, cold and wet ~
But I bring thee a Sussex rose
    To light your requiem,
Across the Downs to London Town,
    Just for you . . . Sweet Em.

Stanley John Arber

Abstruce Tree

Abstruce tree in pale moonlight
standing grandeur in splendour, depict of might,
your physical silhouette so true so mystic
maturing in wisdom to prevail majestic,
primed to partake, the tree and its spirit
engage in communion on intimate pivot.
Contentment in nook is realised,
tree spirit so comely it's memorised.

P A Wilde

Forces Of Nature

I can see through your heart
    To your soul
The water of life flows the
    Forces of your nature
I can feel you in all
    Your essence
Whenever you breeze by
    I am touched by your presence

On the crest of your shores
    The Messiah of light shines down
On your natural beauty
    Burning crimson and gold
I can hear the sights and sounds
    That are all around
Filling me with warmth
    In the rays of your smile
Your fragile body keeps moving
    Breathing ever eternally

You change your colours
    For all to share
The mountains of your strength
    Rise up for all to admire
In all your many emotions
    That you display
None are more beautiful
    And imposing than the forces of your nature.

Matthew Lindley

The Great Outdoors

Freedom of unlimited space
Always comes up ace
Fresh air on my face
Quickens my hear a pace

The tops of my walking boots
Become dampened by the sparkling droplets of early morning dew
The warmth of the rising sun creates a reddened live hue
Spreading warm rays until it gracefully sets at the end of the day

The ever changing views I see are my personal photographs
They will always remain alive as my personal memories
I am spared from arranging my photographs
In albums which become dusty and musty

Busy buzzing pollinating bees
Butterflies dancing horses prancing
The wonderful sound of the waking birds
Dawn chorus draw my eyes up to *look* at the swirls
Fresh morning sky a contrast of white
And clear blue sky the cloud formation changes
From snowy mountains melting into rivers and
Winter seas tossing spuming white pillows

Look up to the clear night sky
Full of twinkling diamonds
The man in the moon is sometimes
There for all to view, just *look* up
These pictures are all *free*
They are *given* by mother nature
Use them carefully so that they are
allowed to mature not taken away by man

Above all the great outdoors *gives*
Us the appreciation and qualities of two
Senses which cannot be conveyed in
Any other way
The sweet succulent *smell* of all
Spring and summer flowers
The *smell* of the salty sea at the
Seaside
The appreciation of the *touch* of the soft
Warm sand under my feet
Contrasting to the coolness of a refreshing dip
Mind the crabs don't nip

The great outdoors *gives* our bodies
An extra bonus
Mental and physical stimulation improves
A general feeling of well being and preservation

Mary Wood

The Lakeside Walk

A perfect place with
Trees to climb on,
Trees to shelter under,
Dry from the mountain mist
The low hung cloud
That clings to Donard
Is lightening,
Trying to let
A little brightness
Even sunshine in!

Margaret Boles

Blesséd Rain

Oh! Lovely heavenly blesséd rain
Making all things fresh again,
The crackéd earth no longer there
All nature bows its head in prayer.

The grassy patch once sparse and brown
Now carpeted in a soft green down,
Thistles blowing time away
While welcoming a new-born day.

Flowers opening petals wide
Welcoming bees to come inside,
Leaves a-rustling in the breeze
Teasing, softly blowing trees.

Insects, scurrying to and fro
Humming, buzzing as they go,
Birds on high in merry note
Warbling sweetly in full throat.

Dear Lord, from whom all blessings come,
Who knows our needs, and guides us home;
Thank You, for the refreshing rain
Making us all feel new again.

Madge Goodman

The Return

I strolled through the countryside, on a peaceful summer's day,
and the farmers they were busy, in the fields, making hay.
The cows the cud were chewing, the sheep gave their gentle bleat,
it was wonderful to feel again, the grass beneath my feet.

I walked down by the river, and heard the familiar sounds,
of the water running, over stones in leaps and bounds.
A sudden flash of silver, as a fish darted away,
from a blue Kingfisher, as it dived to catch its prey.

The fields of golden buttercups, and cowslips here and there,
and the gentle breeze that carried, their fragrance on the air.
All of these brought memories of my younger days,
when I worked in the fields in the summer, making hay.

Ploughing, sowing and reaping, tilling the fertile land,
strolling home at the end of the day, with tired feet, and blistered
                                                                hand.
But one day I'll come back again and this time, I will stay,
no more to search for fortunes in the cites, far away.
For here I need no fortune, no need to pay a fee,
because life's most precious things, are here, and they are free.

Johann K S Brangham-Tucker

On Sketching

As I would seek something of the day
To depict one moment
I could trace as a pencil on a paper
Its consequence but a line on the page
Its significance in how well it was put down on the page
Of what is represented
In front of me
Adept in its thread
To what I have seen
On this journey
On its account
If pencil put to paper
The passing image
My ramble through the countryside
My sketch
My record and journal of the day
As such I have spent
On this excursion
Myself part of this world
As travelling I see
Of green fields
Grazing cattle
Trees and woods also
I am in the outside
The fresh air
In life
I would find in this something for me
In sketching in the countryside.

J Bayless

A Visit To Kelmscott

I trod the road from Lechlade
    With a pilgrim's pride:
My goal the shrine of Kelmscott
    Hugging riverside.

The day was dry and dusty,
    Early in July,
And I hot with excitement,
    With impatient eye.

I passed the church, a building
    Quaint, upon my road,
The Post, the Plough, each private,
    Quiet, restful abode.

Then to the ancient manor
    Down towards the Thames,
The house where William Morris
    Penned poetic gems.

Behind the antique windows
    Of his chosen room,
He dreamt of Utopia,
    Working on his loom.

Contented now, I rested
    Underneath a tree
With sun that smiled on Morris
    Smiling down at me.

I thought of dark-eyed Janey
    When Rossetti's muse.
The painter, not the husband,
    Cupid made her choose.

    F G Ward

Rollers

Whilst wandering beside the ocean waves,
The mind turns to those who had earlier found a watery grave.
The ozone air is so very bracing,
But as you saunter slowly you soon find your pulse is racing.

You may stop a while to survey the view
Great rollers can be seen and they could be of use to you.
If you have a vivid imagination,
You can think of them being sea-horses chasing each other from
station to station.

Those sea-horses have a white mane,
But you see many pretty blues all the same.
It can be great fun, seeing a different scene,
And takes one's mind off what might have been.

Nearer the shore can be seen smaller waves,
Lapping softly but always trying to behave.
They hum their own little tune,
But they hope to be like the big ones soon.

Betty Green

Untitled

The trees in orchards everywhere,
Tell us again, that autumn's here,
Their heavy laden branches sway
With pears, and ruddy apples gay,
Filberts lie thick upon the ground,
In meadows green, the mushroom's found,
Blackberries there, on bush so thick
Are free, for everyone to pick,
The majesty of trees so tall,
Mosses and ivy on the wall,
Thistle heads floating in the breeze,
Food for little Goldfinch, these,
Grey Squirrel scrambles noisily,
Nimbly he jumps from tree to tree,
Nuts and acorns gathers he,
His winter store to multiply.

Lily Page

Goodbye Summer

The end of our Summer, is drawing near
Those bright blue skies, are not so clear
Sultry nights, we won't see again
Replaced by dark days, and showers of rain
A glimpse of the Sun, on occasions you'll see
The Season is changing, quite naturally
The leaves on the trees, confirm that's true
Many fall to the ground, after changing their hue
A cold sly wind, puts a nip in the air
Those Sun brown limbs, are no longer bare
So Goodbye to our Summer, that's history now
Autumn is waiting, eagerly, to make her bow.

Joseph Bottrell

Woodland Magic

A sudden hush hangs in the air.
And circles in the woodlands over there.
No breath of wind disturbs the trees.
No lightest touch to move the leaves.
No sudden sound.
No softest footsteps disturb the ground.
No screech of owls, no wings of bats.
A mist that rises from the ground.
To swirl about and drift around.
But wait, did I hear the faintest sound.
To venture deep into these woods.
And head toward a quiet glade.
And even in this darkness.
No sense of being afraid.
The moon then breaks from out the clouds.
A shaft of light filters through the trees.
To penetrate this darkest night.
To shed its light on a hidden place.
And reveal a wonderful sight.
A female deer had given birth this darkest night.
And as you gaze in rapturous awe.
As the mother cleans this baby fawn.
That came before the early dawn.
And if out walking with your dog.
On some other quiet night.
And hear those faint and strangest sounds.
Take care but don't take flight.
Just venture deeper into this wood.
And look for that warm soft magical light.
Because in these woodlands deep.
When most birds and creatures are fast asleep.
The most beautiful things can occur at night.

Tom Usher

Time

As the train winds on through hill and dale
'It' blows too like a passing gale
As a sea-bound craft is tossed by waves
'It' goes unnoticed through echoless caves.

The silence can be heard, it is so loud
Like the sea's white surf, like the sky's bright cloud,
Like the rustling of leaves in a still-standing tree
Or a soaring eagle in the air, so free.

Nature continues through winter and spring
No matter what man or beast may bring,
It's an old but true saying regardless of all
That time stands still for no man at all.

In the light of this we all must beware
To be ready for when Christ comes in the air,
There'll be a loud trumpet call and a great shout
When Christ's will join Him, both lawyer and lout.

G M Archer

Summer's Daily Round

Wings of the morning emerging from night
Crystal-clear dewdrops in pale golden light.
Mid-morning recess, the sun climbs the sky:
Elevenses' coffee with gooseberry pie.

Fiery and glowing the sun overhead,
Warmth and contentment for our daily bread,
Heat of the noon-day to nourish the grain;
Afternoon tea-time with cream cakes and plain.

Cool of the evening and rose-petal scent,
Eventide whisperings the breezes invent.
Night-time comes slowly and shadows appear,
Crossing one's thoughts, fancy flickers a fear.

Midnight when witches cavort in the wood
Casting their spells but doing no good.
Two in the morning, if you're still awake,
There's no time to sleep for it's nearly daybreak.

Frank Ede

Mother Earth

Human nature cloaks many a surprise
and the characteristics of man are numerous.
As the sun and moon cast their rays
and the seasons fulfil nature's calendar ~ quietly and miraculously
the lives of many are coloured vividly ~ richly and inescapably.

Many suffer from terror or hardship
so the inexplicable in life gives misery.
Yet the globe has warm hearts
and such fine people can restore empty loneliness ~ serenely and
                                                    unpretentiously.

Fortunes waiver, great shadows are seen
yet the unbelievable sign of life emerges.
A new dawn brings hope, care and joy:
So all creatures respond, giving gloriously ~ energy and personality.
That touch of humour and strength always envelops ~ kindly yet
                                                    perspicuously.

Margaret Ann Wheatley

The Summer Sun

The sun is shining on my face,
Holding me in its warm embrace,
Giving my skin a healthy glow,
That only outdoor people know.

Alas a breeze decides to stray,
Where my sunbeams are at play,
Cooling my skin I may decide,
Perhaps it's time I went inside.

Once again, in a different place,
The sun is shining on my face,
So hot my skin begins to leak,
Is this the pleasure that I seek?

My healthy glow I fear may turn,
Into some painful sunburn,
Once again I may decide,
Perhaps it's time to go inside.

P A Kelly

Winter

Cold, wind, rain, sleet,
Bare trees, slippery paths,
Dark nights and frosty mornings ~
Is that all that Winter has to offer?

Then what about the bright lights,
Stars in the sky and warm, glowing fires?
Wrapping-paper, Christmas cards,
Tinsel, fir trees and carol choirs?
Bright, woolly jumpers, hats and scarves,
Hot, buttered toast, cocoa, mince pies,
Satsumas and oranges, turkey and stuffing;
Sleigh-bells, snowmen, robins, holly,
Father Christmas all fat and jolly;
Carol-services and Salvation Army bands
Hailing a Saviour born in a far-off land!
Then when all that is over we can still dance and sing,
For with the close of Winter comes the beginning of Spring!

Kathy Rawstron

Magical Seasons

Joyous seasons abound they are heralded and made clear
With intimate feelings they surround year after year
Many are the favourites to behold as their secrets unfold
Of many treasured memories their stories they are told
Of Spring that gay harbinger reveals an awakening life
Gone is all that misery where once so dreary causing strife
Sweet scented blossoms now invade the air
With this great awakening with the Spring we too might share

Summer hazy idyllic days lounging in pleasant sunshine
Gentle wafting of the breeze such a delicious past-time
Nature perfected this season and with abundance poured
All her wondrous love and glory that within our memory is stored
Autumn of our sheer delight as colours change rapidly
Sunshine plays an important part creating nature's tapestry
Woodlands carpeted with a display of glorious fallen leaves
Wearily all must now decline as the next season proceeds

Winter brisk that brings a chill over forests plains and hills
All being safely gathered in as frosts emerges and spins
Beautiful pictures now unfold more than an artist could ever capture
Here the season then reverts to another chapter
Joyous as those seasons abound throughout our life time true
As they proceed in revolving around introducing many things new
Older we have grown and a little more set we then evoke our
pleasurable dreams
Unto each season those many secrets are kept as we hold all in high
esteem

R D Hiscoke

Ode To A Race Track

I'm getting all excited as I dress in casual wear
My friends will be here shortly to transport me over there
I look around to finally check that I've got everything
Then grab my purse and then my coat and lastly my keyring
I'm looking out the window to get a better view
I'll know the car when it arrives, it's a slatey colour blue
Ah there they are, I see them now, coming around the bend
Now all I have to think about is how much I will spend
I lock my door and run around to get into the back
Now we're off to have a day at the local banger track
Hot dog stalls and burger bars are dotted around the stands
Cars come in on trailers and are careful to avoid the fans
Engines roar and tyres scream and dust flies all around
I take my place amongst the throng and listen to the sounds
Crash and bang and wallop, the back's just been caved in
It no more resembles a motorcar but looks like a dustbin
The race is stopped, we hold our breath with wonder and with fright
Minutes pass and then we see the driver is all right
And so the afternoon wears on, we watch race after race
And we don't mind what weather comes, there is no better place.

Virginia Barrasin

The Granite Horse

A creature of whom I am very fond
Is a Granite Horse.
It sits all day by the duck pond
(It isn't real of course!)

Did someone chisel you into that form,
Or nature shape your style?
At what place were you first born,
Have you travelled many a mile?

Do you enjoy the sights you see?
The ducks and swans a-floating.
Would you prefer to be more free
And not have people gloating?

Children ride your back and fantasise,
To them you are quite real.
They sit astride and realise
You have your own appeal.

Your back is hard to straddle,
But curves in the right place,
You wear no leather saddle,
Just bear a horsey face.

Trees surround you everywhere,
Cars pull up alongside.
You can only sit and stare,
Can you this life abide?

Do you gallop in the night
When the moon is bright and round?
Do you feel like Pegasus in flight
Instead of on the ground?

What do you think about, Stone Horse,
Sitting there all day?
I could meet with you, of course,
And simply fly away!

Julia Trevarthen

The Snowfall

The snow started light but soon covered every marking on the land,
It covered up the weeds, the mud and rubbish left by Man.
It covered every small glade and casually worked and sowed,
Its thick white crystal carpets in frozen shapes all of its own.
It slowly kept on coming down all through the long, still night,
Until with morning's early rays it stopped its random flights.
And as dawn began the new day and folks looked from their homes,
All they could see was whiteness wrapped in a coat of thickened
                                                            snow.

Nature's way had bathed then cleansed every blemish on the scene,
A perfect Christmas picture etched in a white Angelic frieze.
If only what had happened could always stay that way,
A painting done at nightime where snowdrifts had chose to play.
Just for those brief dark hours Nature coated every hill,
A scene of peace and quiet as the night lay very still.
It meant for once on Christmas Day ~ not only in a song,
White Christmas dreamed by singers had truly come along.

Paul Sanders

How Green Was My England

How green was my England in childhood days
As we romped over meadow and lea
Those long hot summers of yesteryear
Brought joy and freedom to me

We walked in the shade of a leafy lane
And played by a babbling brook
The flowers that grew on the river bank
Formed a picture of pleasure to look

The cattle grazed in fields of green
The yellow corn swayed in the breeze
We'd gaze upon this idyllic scene
As the birds sang high in the trees

The hedgerows aglow with blossom and berry
The streams all crystal and clear
Wildlife abound where ever we looked
A rabbit, a badger, a deer

Covered now by concrete and brick
As the motor car fouls the air
No fruit bearing trees, no grass on the fields
Just built up, barren and bare

Gone are my pictures of childhood days
Never more to be seen
I still love my England, this land of my birth
But I remember when it was green

V K Cook

Clyde Walkway

Woodsmoke drifts on concrete
River churning curds of foam
Seagulls conning ducks of casted crusts
Dipped in a drowned cathedral
Dinky red bus on the bridge
Man on a bench
Leftover.
Woman fishing phrases with a song and a prayer
Sunday worship.

Jess Dalrymple

Nature

The bird spreads its wings
Like a tree does its branches.
They both need food and water
To survive and sing.

Listen to the birds
When they sing,
Listen to the trees
Rustling in the wind.

Birds feed their young
Just like the trees its leaves.
Gently letting them go
When the time comes to do so.

Trees last longer
But life goes on.
New growth or new life
Whatever nature decides.

Birds greatest fear is cats
Killing them and their young.
A trees greatest fear is man
Killing them by cutting them down.

Margaret Smith

Seasons

Winter is beauty asleep,
When the bud is a scar on the stem,
And the stem is edged with diamonds
Bright in the pale sun
And the sun in a pale sky.

Spring clothes the trees in golden green,
The blackbird claims his home in song;
Small flowers lie low
And star the ground.

Summer is rich, abounding
In bloom and colour and light
Rivers are slow under hanging boughs
Beauty is heavy with leaf
And hot in the sun.

Autumn has richness too
With fruits and tawny trees,
With mists that lie in the valleys
And cooler air,
And brown earth.

We need all the seasons,
One alone would pall.
Sleep, hope, languor and maturity,
All are given.

Mary Pickford

Summer Beauty

The season of the year most enjoyed, is summer,
Watching everything come alive from their wintry slumber.
Trees of all kinds, budding out into different shaped leaves.
Tulips, daffodils, hyacinths blooming till their fullness they achieve.

Blue skies of sculptured, cottony clouds, all so clear,
Make me think of tomorrow, another glorious day so near.
Daytime, appears a huge ball of golden sun among the clouds, so
                                          high up there,
Nightime, radiates the light from the moon and stars,
Though darkness surrounds them everywhere.

Summer, a time for families to come together,
Going on vacations, and picnics in the is energizing weather.
Voices of young and old, chattering to their heart's content,
Planning the next day's agenda, so every day is well spent.

Water being put to use especially on its hottest days,
Refreshing everyone and everything, in whatever way.
Now and then, showers of raindrops pitter patter,
Nourishing all creation, thirsting to rejuvenate an appearance, torn
                                          and tattered.

Birds soaring the wide blue yonder,
Flapping their wings, peacefully, I gaze and ponder.
Chirping sounds of Cardinals, Blue Jays and cooing doves,
Summer, a great time of the year, I really love.

Christine Swetland Rakoczy

The Warning

Whilst out walking one fine summer's day
Amongst the smell of new-mown hay
I stopped to look around and stare
The beauty God and nature provided for me there
Graceful butterflies colourful wings when spread
Poppies in cornfields proudly showing off their red
Swallows swooping and feeding on speeding wings
Kingfishers diving Oh! The joy of hearing nightingales sing
To see trout take a fly on a fast-running stream
When the pace of life was slow and one could dream
Amongst the peace of rustling leaves
Singing you a tune played on a gentle breeze
Walk woods that were filled with Primrose and cuckoo flowers
That scented your nostrils after springtime showers
When rooks built nests in trees so high
Cackling ducks and geese seen silhouetted in a moonlit sky
Meadows that were once filled with different grasses
The startled cry of a pheasant when a stranger passes
Nature has changed its weather giving us a *warning*
Stop pollution and spraying and global warming
Beware if we don't there'll be nothing left to save
Buried forever in a man-made grave.

R Cousins

Roman Steps

We can see you on this crispy blue late
October day walking through our mountains
on steps you call Roman. That far-flung state,
once the world's imperial mast, maintains

it set the route. But we showed those Romans
the way: they just built the road and Goth slaves
did the hard work: broke rocks non-humans
forged in canyons and caves, and cut the staves.

They had heard about our superfine gold
and, eager to bedeck their Lucretias and Fabiolas
and the Emperor's favourite mistress, sold
us in search of the largest fistulas.

Resplendent metal from these desert crags
at Claudius' limits of domination
adorned the eternal city's marble flags
and shone on southern imagination.

We return into the dark stones and rocks
of this windswept heather-clad wilderness
and let him who, laughing, denies or mocks
our lives feel this region's winter coldness.

By herds of goats and swirling falcons
they may sense that worth which comes not from men
but from the planet: not from false icons
But from the sky and the earth's long amen.

Francis Pettitt

Peep At Nature

I see Nature through an ice-glazed window,
Green blades of grass, standing to attention, sharp as razors.
Red as robin's breast are the berries on the trees.
Silver nets across my window this spider's web
Moves gentle in the breeze.
Leaves will dance and spin around
As they skip along the ground.
Flowers painted in my garden by a rainbow brush
Cat curled up fast asleep
She has a peep at Nature,
Then falls back to sleep.

Jane Treloar

Natures Way

And so the little seed grew beside the shimmering silver pool
A vibrant crown upon its head like Natures precious jewel
Flowers nod in the gentle breeze releasing their fragrant fumes
Neighbouring trees sway in harmony shaking their magnificent
plumes
Their branches are laden with summer fruit that fall upon the mossy
ground
Wings of the birds distantly hum their singing a wonderful resound

And so the little seed grew in the ancient swamps of the lowland
Stretching its quivering branches like a childs enquiring hand
Mists are swirling from the waters that obscure the valiant oak
A battle with the stagnant weeds that drag to maim and choke
Deathly lonliness rules the moor with only the wind to shriek and
howl
And poison manifests within the roots resting its aching bowel

(Some are fortunate when others are not such is Natures way!)

J Hogan